COUNCIL *on*
FOREIGN
RELATIONS

Council Special Report No. 96
September 2023

Rethinking International Rules on Subsidies

Jennifer A. Hillman and Inu Manak

The Council on Foreign Relations (CFR) is an independent, nonpartisan membership organization, think tank, and publisher dedicated to being a resource for its members, government officials, business executives, journalists, educators and students, civic and religious leaders, and other interested citizens in order to help them better understand the world and the foreign policy choices facing the United States and other countries. Founded in 1921, CFR carries out its mission by maintaining a diverse membership, with special programs to promote interest and develop expertise in the next generation of foreign policy leaders; convening meetings at its headquarters in New York and in Washington, DC, and other cities where senior government officials, members of Congress, global leaders, and prominent thinkers come together with Council members to discuss and debate major international issues; supporting a Studies Program that fosters independent research, enabling CFR scholars to produce articles, reports, and books and hold roundtables that analyze foreign policy issues and make concrete policy recommendations; publishing *Foreign Affairs*, the preeminent journal on international affairs and U.S. foreign policy; sponsoring Independent Task Forces that produce reports with both findings and policy prescriptions on the most important foreign policy topics; and providing up-to-date information and analysis about world events and American foreign policy on its website, CFR.org.

The Council on Foreign Relations takes no institutional positions on policy issues and has no affiliation with the U.S. government. All views expressed in its publications and on its website are the sole responsibility of the author or authors.

Council Special Reports (CSRs) are policy briefs, produced to provide a rapid response to a developing crisis or contribute to the public's understanding of current policy dilemmas. CSRs are written by individual authors—who may be CFR fellows or acknowledged experts from outside the institution—in consultation with an advisory committee, and are intended to take sixty days from inception to publication. The committee serves as a sounding board and provides feedback on a draft report. It usually meets twice—once before a draft is written and once again when there is a draft for review; however, advisory committee members, unlike Task Force members, are not asked to sign off on the report or to otherwise endorse it. Once published, CSRs are posted on CFR.org.

For further information about CFR or this Special Report, please write to the Council on Foreign Relations, 58 East 68th Street, New York, NY 10065, or call the Communications office at 212.434.9888. Visit our website, CFR.org.

To submit a letter in response to a Council Special Report for publication on our website, CFR.org, you may send an email to publications@cfr.org. Alternatively, letters may be mailed to us at: Publications Department, Council on Foreign Relations, 58 East 68th Street, New York, NY 10065. Letters should include the writer's name, postal address, and daytime phone number. Letters may be edited for length and clarity, and may be published online. Please do not send attachments. All letters become the property of the Council on Foreign Relations and will not be returned. We regret that, owing to the volume of correspondence, we cannot respond to every letter.

CONTENTS

FOREWORD

International trade rules constraining governments' subsidies use date back to the Tokyo Round negotiations of the General Agreement on Tariffs and Trade in the 1970s. At the time, the United States pushed for restraints on subsidies use by governments that could distort competition for U.S. firms at home and abroad. Other governments—including those of Japan and many European and developing countries—wanted to regulate the United States' ability to slap "countervailing" duties on imports it considered unfairly subsidized. The Agreement on Subsidies and Countervailing Measures was among the hardest-fought compromises in the negotiations that led to the creation of the World Trade Organization (WTO) in 1995.

However, the practical results of those agreements have been disappointing. Although these disciplines provided a novel roadmap for identifying and remedying subsidy activities, they were mostly honored in the breach. In this report, two Council on Foreign Relations experts—Jennifer A. Hillman, senior fellow for trade and international political economy, and Inu Manak, fellow for trade policy—describe how the rules did little to prevent widespread industrial subsidies use by countries hoping to gain an edge in international trade. China's state-owned enterprises, in particular, largely sidestepped the restrictions, and the penalties imposed for violations were too weak to be a real deterrent. Over time, many countries ignored even the most basic transparency obligations by refusing to notify the WTO of the type and scale of subsidies they were offering. The failure of the WTO to constrain industrial subsidies has played no small role in generating U.S. frustration with the organization, which has left its dispute settlement function crippled.

Enter the Joe Biden administration, which has flipped the script by embracing the most expansive subsidies use in modern U.S. history with the passage of the Inflation Reduction Act and the Chips and Science Act. The stated goals of these laws are to accelerate the transition to cleaner energy and slow climate change and to strengthen the U.S. ability to compete with China. Japan, the European Union, and others are following suit with their own subsidy programs, which are raising questions about the nature and future of subsidy disciplines. While there are compelling justifications for these initiatives, as Hillman and Manak write, a subsidies competition could "stifle innovation, create substantial inefficiencies, exacerbate the concentration of corporate power, waste precious taxpayer funds, and fuel crony capitalism." To address these risks, they call for a concerted effort to reform international subsidies rules to permit benign uses—such as fighting climate change—while reducing predatory competition.

In particular, the authors recommend new arrangements modeled after the WTO Agreement on Agriculture (AoA), which helped cabin the competition between the United States and Europe to heap subsidies on their farmers. The AoA had two crucial innovations: capping the overall size of subsidies and distinguishing among harmful, trade-distorting subsidies; minimally distortive subsidies; and subsidies with important social purposes. The first category is restricted while the latter two remain largely unregulated. Similar principles, the authors argue, should frame a new agreement on industrial subsidies: an overall cap on trade-distorting subsidies, with exceptions for those that support research and development, clean energy and global health efforts, and assistance to developing countries. Measures bolstering transparency and compliance would also have to be at the heart of a new deal. Such an agreement would certainly be challenging to negotiate, especially given the current level of distrust between China and the West, but Hillman and Manak offer a thoughtful blueprint for how the gains from such restraints would more than offset the costs.

The United States has been reluctant to show global leadership on international trade for the past several years, but these proposals offer a strong menu for changing course. If industrial policy is to play an increased role in economic strategy going forward, now is the time to consider sensible guardrails to prevent an ensuing arms race in subsidization. A failure to do so could ultimately produce suboptimal outcomes for U.S. competitiveness and other unintended consequences.

Michael Froman
Council on Foreign Relations
September 2023

ACKNOWLEDGMENTS

This Council Special Report is the result of the authors' conviction that a paradigm shift is occurring in the world of international trade, with countries around the world shedding their concerns over adherence to trade rules and economic doctrine cautioning against the overuse of domestic subsidies—and that the United States is leading the shift through the enactment of large subsidy programs that could provoke trade disputes, invite imitation, or both. Either way, the stage has been set for a new era of industrial policies that merit serious consideration in terms of the implications for long-standing trade rules and practices that separated the unfair from the justified and the subsidized from the market-oriented.

We would like to thank the trade experts and economists who generously shared their time, ideas, written work, and expertise with us along with way. We are particularly grateful to Charlene Barshefsky, Raj Bhala, Renee Bowen, Chad Bown, Jonathan E. Colby, Bernard Hoekman, Simon Lester, Bill Reinsch, Luca Rubini, Joel Trachtman, and Mark Wu. Their insights and guidance strengthened our work at every turn.

This report would not have been possible without the support of many people at CFR. We thank former CFR President Richard Haass for recognizing the importance and significance of the shifts occurring around trade and industrial policy and for giving us the opportunity to coauthor this report. We also thank CFR Director of Studies Jim Lindsay for his gentle nudges, insights, and perseverance in getting this report across the finish line. We thank Patricia Dorff, Cassandra Jensen, and the Publications team for editing and preparing the report for publication. CFR's Digital Services team deserves recognition for designing and producing the excellent graphics that appear in this report. We want to thank two research associates, Alex Tippet and Gabriel Cabanas, for their research support at the beginning and end of this project. Finally, special thanks to the Friedman Family Foundation Strategic Innovation Fund at CFR for supporting the work of Inu Manak, and to the Renewing America initiative, which is supported by the Bernard and Irene Schwartz Foundation.

Jennifer A. Hillman
Inu Manak

INTRODUCTION

The United States has long considered "industrial policy"—meaning government action that encourages or directly subsidizes the expansion of certain economic sectors over others—as anathema, verging on socialism, or worse. In the face of the COVID-19 pandemic, global supply-chain disruptions, climate change, and the rise of China, however, what was once off the table has come front and center. The Joe Biden administration's embrace of industrial policy means the United States is back in the business of providing major inducements to invest in strategically important segments of the economy.

That shift has prompted cries from across the globe that the United States is fostering unfair competition and breaking the rules it helped shape as part of the World Trade Organization (WTO). Responding to complaints from Europe that the scale of financing available only for "made in America" products will undermine European competitiveness by driving European companies across the Atlantic, the Biden team urges Europe to subsidize its own producers. To those contending that $805 billion in subsidies for semiconductor manufacturing and research, climate and energy investments, and infrastructure spending make U.S. economic policy look suspiciously like the Chinese policies of state dominance and support that Washington has been railing against for years, Biden's chief trade negotiator, U.S. Trade Representative (USTR) Katherine Tai, asserts that American subsidies are "a product of a democratic rule-of-law system" and are "meant to operate in a market system to influence firm behavior." To the extent that the subsidies are directed at fighting climate change, the Biden administration contends that it deserves kudos that the United States is finally putting serious resources into greening the U.S. economy.[1]

Coming on the heels of a polycrisis, the perception of countries' urgent need to build up their resiliency in critical goods and services, coupled with the existential threat of climate change, means that moving toward industrial policies and increasing subsidies is warranted and indeed essential. However, the urgency of the problems does not mean abandoning well-founded concerns that industrial policy—done wrong—can stifle innovation, create substantial inefficiencies, exacerbate the concentration of corporate power, waste precious taxpayer funds, and fuel crony capitalism. Nor does the immediacy of acting diminish concerns that major increases in using subsidies can harm smaller countries that cannot compete with the government largesse of the United States, China, or the European Union (EU), and will drive up trade tensions if the subsidies discriminate or violate basic WTO rules.

The central concern today is how to craft industrial and subsidies policy in a way that will minimize trade frictions and distortions while maximizing the common good.[2] To do that, the current rules governing using subsidies should be rethought and revitalized. Such efforts should begin with improving subsidies' transparency. Beyond procedural reforms, major global actors should embrace limits on the total amount of industrial subsidies they will grant, along with certain clearly defined exclusions. To ensure that such subsidy disciplines are adhered to, policymakers should expand the penalties for violating the rules. An updated subsidies regime could go a long way toward preventing a costly and divisive subsidy war while encouraging needed investments in climate change technology and supply-chain resilience.

A GLOBAL
SUBSIDIES RACE

The United States supported international rules in response to the troubling rise of subsidies in the 1960s and 1970s. When the Agreement on Subsidies and Countervailing Measures (SCM Agreement) was being negotiated, the United States was, unsurprisingly, pushing for its successful adoption, not least because many of the provisions concerning a primary discipline on subsidies—countervailing duties (CVDs)—were based on U.S. law and practice. Fast-forward to today, and a different view toward subsidies is taking shape that is both positive and strikingly bipartisan.[3] Concerns about the inadequacy of existing institutions to deal with global crises, such as pandemics and climate change, coupled with China's rise—and with it the rise of state intervention and non-market measures—has increased calls for a U.S. response.

The Donald Trump administration's approach was to put "America first," which meant, for instance, prioritizing the domestic production of COVID-19 vaccines with little coordination on a global vaccine rollout.[4] Then, in an attempt to discipline China on trade, Trump applied tariffs on billions of dollars of Chinese imports and negotiated a deal for China to increase purchases of U.S. goods (which fell far short of expectations).[5] Even with a change of administrations, the impetus behind those actions did not fade. In fact, trade policy itself is increasingly intertwined with industrial policy, and although the tool of choice can vary, subsidies are growing in importance.

THE BIRTH OF A NEW U.S. INDUSTRIAL POLICY

Industrial policy generally refers to government efforts to promote specific industries that policymakers have identified as critical for national security or economic competitiveness. As CFR Senior Fellow Edward Alden observes, "It's about the government putting a thumb on the scale, rather than just assuming that market outcomes are going to produce the maximum benefit."[6] The type of intervention pursued can take several forms, such as subsidies, tariffs, regulations, tax incentives, government procurement rules, and preferred access to credit. Industrial policy is also motivated by various objectives, including economic competitiveness, fostering infant industries, national security, or protectionism.

Although the United States has historically preferred market-based measures to encourage economic activity, the debate over government intervention through industrial policy has deep roots. The U.S. experience with industrial policy stretches back to the country's founding, when the young nation's leaders debated the best ways to help economically develop a largely agrarian market that depended on imports from foreign manufacturers. Back then, the United States relied heavily on tech transfer from Great Britain to modernize industry. That reliance motivated Alexander Hamilton to write his *Report on Manufacturers* in 1791, in which he called for the support of infant industries that provided for the "the essentials of national supply," including "the means of subsistence habitation, clothing and defence."[7] However, Hamilton understood the economics of such a policy, as well as the unintended consequences that could result, which is precisely why he did not favor tariffs as a tool of industrial policy; instead, he supported limited use of "bounties" (subsidies) because, compared to tariffs, they were "a more direct and positive type of encouragement" and "did not create scarcity and raise domestic prices."[8]

Hamilton was also aware that expansive use of subsidies could generate economic harm. He suggested support for only a limited number of new industries (i.e., coal, raw wool, sailcloth, cotton, and glass). In fact, Hamilton was averse to supporting "long established" industries, which he suggested "must almost always be of questionable policy."[9] However, facing opposition from Congress, particularly from the Jeffersonian Republicans, Hamilton's narrow idea for using limited subsidies would not become official policy. Later, Presidents Thomas Jefferson and James Madison would support the idea of subsidies as manufacturing interests aligned with the Republicans. In putting that idea into action, Madison favored an industrial policy that mixed two separate tools: protective tariffs and subsidies.

Today, a similar approach has taken shape. The Biden administration has maintained and expanded on the Trump administration's tariff policy, defended at the time as helping the United States compete globally against a rising China, by introducing major new subsidy programs.[10] Importantly, the primary motivation for those efforts falls into two buckets—to counter China and to fight climate change. Although those motivators for a renewed U.S. industrial policy appear somewhat divergent, the Biden administration has emphasized that its "American industrial strategy" focuses on one core idea: that "strategic public investments are essential to achieving the full potential of our nation's economy."[11] Ultimately, how the United States implements industrial policy will be the litmus test for whether the administration will follow a restrained view modeled on Hamilton's vision of limited subsidies and open markets or the expansive and beggar-thy-neighbor approach embraced by Jefferson and Madison.

OUTCOMPETING A RISING CHINA

China's rapid and explosive economic rise has rattled the foundations of the global economy and unsettled the traditional great powers as they scramble to adjust to a new reality. However, the problems posed by China's ascent are as varied as the policy options put forward to address them. In his February 2023 State of the Union address, Biden called for unity in "winning the competition with China" and said that he "will make no apologies" for "investing in American innovation, in industries that will define the future, and that China's government is intent on dominating."[12] In its *National Strategy for Advanced Manufacturing*, the Biden administration lays out its vision to "revitalize the manufacturing sector, increase the resilience of U.S. supply chains and national security, invest in R&D, and train Americans for jobs of the future."[13] More than one pathway leads to that future, however, and different visions of what it should look like are beginning to emerge.

Some voices in the administration have called for a strategic and measured approach. Director of the National Economic Council Brian Deese cited Hamilton in his call for reinvigorating U.S. industry but also emphasized that "this is about strategic engagement, not isolationism."[14] Secretary of Commerce Gina Raimondo has struck a similar tone.[15] Treasury Secretary Janet Yellen favored consideration of removing the Trump China tariffs and, in a meeting with China's Vice Premier Liu He, emphasized that the two governments "share a responsibility to show that China and the United States can manage our differences and prevent competition from becoming anything ever near conflict."[16]

In contrast, others have laid out a more Madisonian vision for industrial policy, arguing for strategically using protective tariffs in addition to broad government investment in manufacturing. Katherine Tai, for example, praised the Trump administration's Section 301 tariffs on China, calling them "a significant piece of leverage" and a means of defense to "level the playing field and entice enforcement in other areas."[17] She also advocated for broadening industrial policy to many sectors, stating that "the key to American competitiveness going forward" is to replicate the 2022 CHIPS and Science Act for other industries, "especially ones who are facing really, really stiff competition from economies that are not structured like ours, that are much more focused and state-directed," meaning China.[18]

FIGHTING CLIMATE CHANGE

The second area of focus for the Biden administration's industrial policy is taking action to fight climate change. Biden has been vocal about the link between achieving that goal and government financial support. He has also touted the many domestic benefits of tackling climate change. In a press release announcing new greenhouse gas pollution reduction targets, the White House stated that "creating jobs and tackling climate change go hand in hand."[19] Although Biden has held firm on the importance of the Inflation Reduction Act of 2022 (IRA) to achieving U.S. climate goals in the face of criticism from many allies and trading partners, he has also assured allies that the United States is not turning inward. In fact, in a press conference with French President Emmanuel Macron, Biden stated that the United States would "continue to create manufacturing jobs in America but not at the expense of Europe."[20]

A broader concern is whether the United States has kicked off a global subsidies race in which few countries will have the means to participate. For instance, the International Monetary Fund (IMF) estimates that "public adaptation costs [to climate change] will reach around 0.25 percent of global gross domestic product per year in coming decades," noting that "while such estimates can appear manageable at the global level, they aren't representative of the scale of the challenge faced by many poor and vulnerable countries."[21] Ensuring that the benefits of investments in climate change adaptation and mitigation flow beyond the United States is essential for tackling the climate crisis in the long run, as is the need to ensure, as Executive Vice President for the European Commission Margrethe Vestager cautioned, "that the word 'green' doesn't become a euphemism for a new kind of protectionism."[22]

That tension in policy approaches has sparked discussion on the best ways forward to achieve environmental goals through subsidies. Current actions likely conflict with international trade rules, and the widespread adoption of industrial subsidies could unleash a global trade war as countries enact tit-for-tat measures in retaliation.[23] Although future WTO subsidy disputes are perhaps less likely in the short run due to the lack of a functioning dispute settlement mechanism, a U.S. industrial policy that promotes and protects U.S.–located manufacturing against foreign competition will be seen in the long run as an unnecessary violation of the global rules and could undermine the worthy purpose of the programs.

Furthermore, the Biden administration has often blurred the lines between its two primary motivations for using subsidies—countering China and fighting climate change. Katherine Tai has stated that the IRA's purpose is more than combating climate change: it is also to respond to "a significant distortion" in the global economy brought about by the rise of China.[24] Adding that goal to the fight against climate change also underscores the need for basic guardrails to overcome both insufficiencies in the existing rules and the temptation to try to outcompete China on subsidies. Such a path would be expensive and risks alienating U.S. trading partners whose help the United States currently needs to rein in China's behavior and address shared challenges, especially climate change.

TRADE LAW DISCIPLINES ON SUBSIDIES

Because subsidies are common in most economic sectors, are used by myriad countries for numerous reasons, take many forms, and are provided through national, subnational, and sometimes municipal entities, they have challenged policymakers and trade negotiators for decades.[25] The diverse and widespread nature of subsidies means they have great potential to alter trade and investment flows, detract from the value of tariff bindings and other market access commitments, and undercut public support for open trade if they appear to unfairly privilege exports from the subsidizing country.

A TROUBLED HISTORY

From the 1947 inception of the General Agreement on Tariffs and Trade (GATT), the issue of whether and how to discipline subsidies was divisive.[26] The most that could be agreed upon in 1947 was the language in GATT Article XVI requiring parties to notify the GATT Secretariat of any domestic subsidies that could affect exports, and a more general statement that countries "should seek to avoid" using export subsidies.

Those meager disciplines tightened in the 1973–79 Tokyo Round of negotiations with the adoption of the Subsidies Code.[27] The Code contained provisions making export subsidies (with exceptions for agriculture exports and for developing countries) a per se violation of the rules and added a requirement that countries applying countervailing duties had to first prove that their domestic industry had been injured by subsidized imports.[28] However, not all GATT members joined the Subsidies Code.

The major modernization and expansion of the subsidy rules came from the 1986–93 Uruguay Round of negotiations that ultimately helped create the WTO and with it the Agreement on Subsidies and Counter-vailing Measures. The SCM Agreement applies to all WTO members and includes for the first time a definition of a subsidy, along with notification requirements and a process for overseeing subsidy activities.

WTO DISCIPLINES ON SUBSIDIES

Under WTO rules, companies can be said to receive a "subsidy" only if that subsidy emanates from a government. To avoid having governments set up agencies or bodies to do indirectly what they cannot do directly, Article 1 of the SCM Agreement captures financial contributions not only by "a government" but also by "any public body." In addition, the subsidy definition covers situations where a government "entrusts or directs a private body to carry out one or more of the type of functions" constituting financial contributions by a government. Those contributions include direct transfers of funds (e.g., a loan or loan guarantee); otherwise-due government revenue that is foregone (e.g., tax credits); government provision of goods or services (e.g., provision by government of cheap inputs) or purchasing of goods (e.g., government buying products at above-market rates); or income or price supports.

To be defined as a subsidy, the financial contribution has to confer a "benefit" on the recipient. In general, a benefit is found when the financial contribution leaves a recipient better off than it would otherwise have been absent that contribution, meaning that the recipient is better off than if it had paid market rates for the loans, goods, or services provided by the government. Complications in determining those market rates arise in markets that are distorted, particularly by significant government intervention in "nonmarket" economies such as in China or Vietnam.

For a subsidy (other than a prohibited subsidy) to be actionable (i.e., subject to remedies) under the SCM Agreement, the subsidy needs to be "specific" to an enterprise or industry. That sort of requirement is essential to any subsidies regime because governments participate in wide-ranging activity that is acknowledged as appropriate and desirable, even if it provides a subsidy to local producers, such as for police services or education programs or social security. The SCM Agreement's specificity requirement separates such subsidies from ones that distort trade by favoring certain sectors or enterprises.

The SCM Agreement provides for two distinct remedies to address actionable subsidies. The first and the most common are countervailing duties. CVDs are additional duties that an importing country can apply to future imports to offset the portion of production costs paid for by the subsidy, so long as the subsidized imports have caused demonstrable injury to a domestic industry making a comparable product. The second remedy can be invoked when the competition with subsidized goods takes place in third-country markets or the home market of the subsidizing country. In those instances, a challenge at the WTO can be brought that the subsidies are causing "serious prejudice." Serious prejudice could arise when the subsidy displaces or impedes sales by producers in other countries, or results in price undercutting or price depression or suppression, or results in an increase in the market share of a subsidized commodity product.

WHAT HAS GONE WRONG WITH WTO SUBSIDY DISCIPLINES

The proliferation of global subsidies in the late 1960s and the 1970s generated uneasiness over their economic consequences and helped advance negotiations on the SCM Agreement. The United States was seeking to rein in the growth of subsidies in a number of major trading partners, while much of the rest of the world wanted to limit perceived abuse from excessive U.S. countervailing duties.[29] Historically, the United States is the most frequent global user of CVDs. In fact, of the 289 CVD measures currently in force, the United States accounts for nearly 60 percent. Figure 1 depicts CVD measures in force as of October 2022 by the WTO members imposing them.

Despite the significant and growing number of CVDs imposed by the United States and other WTO countries, concerns persist that the WTO's rules and its dispute settlement system cannot adequately discipline subsidies. Principal among the concerns are the narrow definition of what constitutes a government or public body; the high evidentiary burden in proving the existence of a subsidy; the notification process's failure to provide sufficient transparency; the ineffectiveness of remedies in disciplining subsidies; and the inability of current rules to distinguish between "bad" and "good" subsidies, particularly around those connected to climate change.

NARROW DEFINITION OF GOVERNMENT OR PUBLIC BODY

Companies can be said to receive a "subsidy" only if that subsidy emanates from a "government or a public body." For decades, the United States and other countries applying CVDs took the position that state-owned enterprises (SOEs) fit within the definition of a "public body" if

Figure 1

The United States Is the Largest User of Countervailing Duties

Countervailing duty actions and measures in force by reporting member, October 2022

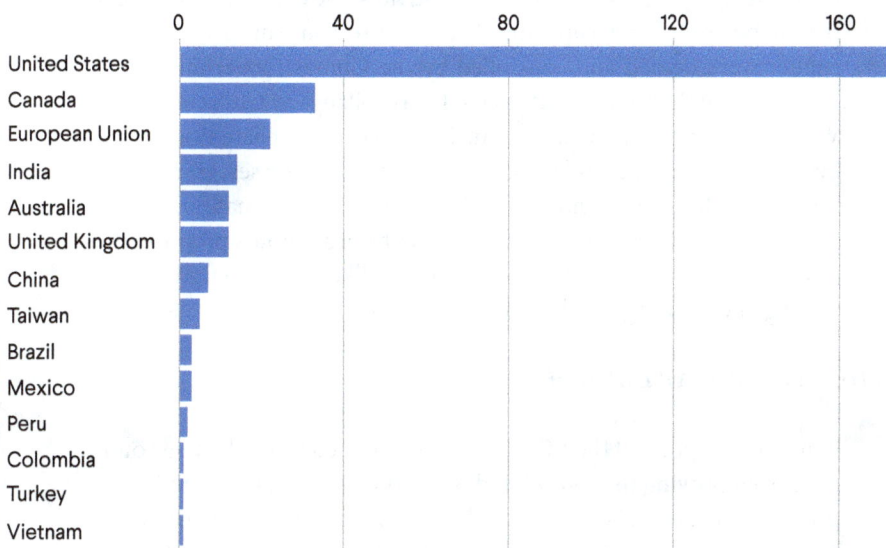

Source: World Trade Organization.

they were government owned or controlled, such that the government could dictate whom to sell to and at what price and thus give a downstream producer an unfair advantage as a result of government provision of goods or services.

The need to police the behavior of SOEs by applying subsidy disciplines is particularly acute in China, given the size and reach of its SOEs. When China joined the WTO in 2001, trade negotiators extracted a commitment from the country "that all state-owned and state-invested enterprises would make purchases and sales based solely on commercial considerations, e.g., price, quality, marketability and availability."[30] For a number of years immediately following China's WTO accession, the Chinese economy appeared on the road to becoming more market-oriented, with a diminished role for SOEs. However, starting in the mid-2000s, China began what has now become a complete U-turn back to a state- and Communist Party–dominated economy.[31]

During this period, the United States began applying the subsidies disciplines and CVDs to imports from China, notwithstanding the nonmarket nature of its economy.[32] China challenged those applications, particularly with respect to its SOEs' activities. In a major ruling related to applying CVDs to off-the-road tires, the U.S. contention that the rubber producers supplying Chinese tire companies with cheap rubber were owned and controlled by the Chinese government and therefore "public bodies" was rejected in a challenge by China under the WTO's dispute settlement system. The WTO's Appellate Body ruled instead that a public body "must be an entity that possesses, exercises or is vested with governmental authority."[33] That decision made imposing CVDs on SOEs, or on products made with cheap inputs produced by SOEs, much more difficult, as few SOEs are likely to be viewed as possessing or exercising governmental authority.

THE EVIDENTIARY BURDEN

Numerous aspects of the SCM Agreement impede complaining countries from proving that prohibited or actionable subsidies were in fact provided. That applies particularly to demonstrating governmental control over an entity to prove it fits within the now narrower definition of a public body; showing that a private entity acted at the "direction" of the government; proving a benchmark against which to judge whether a financial contribution confers a benefit by providing funds or resources at below-market prices; and proving that the subsidies, rather than other factors, caused any adverse effects.

The first two challenges require knowledge of government actions and documentation of what the government did, as well as when and sometimes why. Obtaining such evidence, particularly in nontransparent economies, is extraordinarily difficult, as few government officials put such information into the public record. Moreover, getting domestic firms to provide the necessary evidence to pursue a case is often challenging, either because they fear retaliation or consider turning over business confidential information—even to their own governments—unsafe, especially given heightened concerns about hacking and cyber espionage.

The third challenge is often trickier, as it requires comparisons to a market benchmark, which sometimes does not exist in countries whose government dominates the economy. The last issue—causation—is frequently the hardest, as many factors affect prices, wages, employment, production, and demand. Yet harm caused by factors other than subsidies needs to be separated out to ensure any injury found is properly attributable to subsidized imports.

THE FAILURE OF THE NOTIFICATION PROCESS

One of the significant additions to the subsidies rule book was a requirement that WTO members provide annual notifications of all specific subsidies they have granted or maintained.[34] However, many countries are routinely more than tardy in submitting their notifications. The chair of the WTO's Committee on Subsidies and Countervailing Measures has noted that more than half of WTO members did not submit their 2021 subsidy notifications by the mid-2021 deadline, seventy-six members were more than eighteen months behind, and sixty-five members had not submitted notifications in more than three years. Figure 2 shows the total subsidy notifications made by WTO members to comply with notification requirements under Article 25.1 of the SCM Agreement. The chart shows a growing number of members, now a majority, failing to meet their notification commitments. The opacity on policy actions created by a failure to reveal subsidies presents serious challenges to identifying both inefficiencies and success stories in the grant of subsidies. Furthermore, that lack of transparency contributes to members losing faith in a system where not every country abides equally by the rules.

A major contributor to the problem is the fact that members only notify what they believe to be a subsidy, leaving many programs unidentified. Notifications are also diminished by the narrow definition of what constitutes a public body, meaning that subsidies to SOEs are often underreported. Without clear guidance in the existing rules about what should be notified, little can be done to compel members to justify their missing notifications.

That lack of notifications impairs the SCM Committee's ability to assess member compliance and further limits the breadth of discussions: without a full view of every country's activities, establishing the baseline of global subsidies and an appropriate and measured response to them becomes harder. The WTO, for its part, has recognized the importance of better data and analysis in the subsidies realm and in its currently weak notification process. To that end, it has partnered with the Organization for Economic Co-operation and Development (OECD), the IMF, and the World Bank to create a new online subsidy platform designed to collect the disparate pieces of information on the subsidies used throughout the world and across all major sectors, including agriculture, fossil fuels, fisheries, and industrial sectors. This development is welcome but still requires some degree of government transparency of subsidy data.[35]

THE INEFFECTIVENESS OF THE REMEDIES

Perhaps the biggest impediment to the SCM Agreement's ability to adequately police subsidies derives from the remedies available under WTO rules. The SCM Agreement provides for three different remedies once a subsidy has been found. For prohibited subsidies (those contingent on exports or on using domestic over imported goods), the remedy is to "withdraw the subsidy without delay."[36] For all other subsidies, the SCM Agreement provides two options: imposing countervailing duties if the subsidized goods are entering a member's market and injuring its domestic producers, or commencing a serious prejudice case at the WTO if the damage from trade in the subsidized product is harming the exporting country or a third-country market.

One problem with CVDs is that they are only available in countries that import the product and that have a domestic industry making

Figure 2

The Number of WTO Members Failing to Report Subsidies Has Grown

WTO members by subsidy notification status

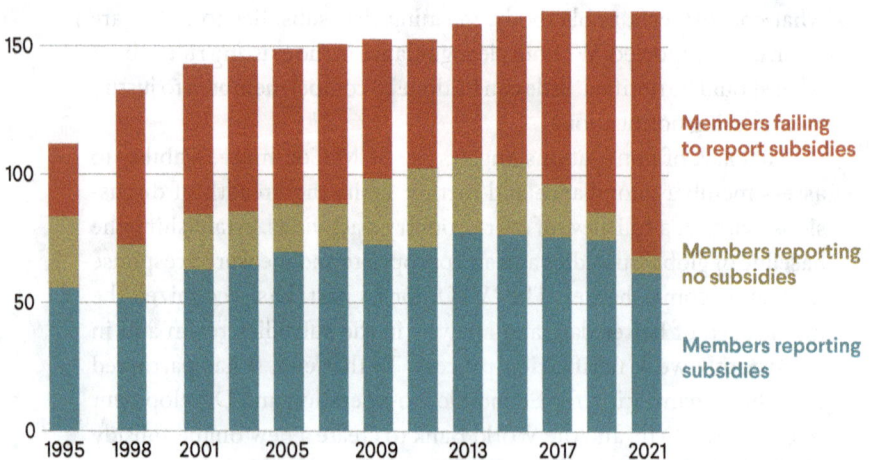

Source: World Trade Organization.

comparable goods. They also require a fairly extensive (and expensive) investigation. Investigating authorities can take a relatively long time to collect the data, investigate the subsidies, and rule on the complaint. Additionally, the investigation often involves extensive solicitation of data from the domestic industry and subsidizing government, with ongoing controversy over its appropriate use and what to do when such information is not forthcoming. Most important, imposing such duties can push the subsidized goods into other markets, thus suppressing prices elsewhere.

The problem with serious prejudice cases is that remedies in the WTO are only prospective. The requirement to "remove the adverse effects of the subsidy" often does little to dismantle the capacity that has been built to produce the subsidized goods in the first place. Moreover, most of the elements of proof of serious prejudice—whether showing displacement in third-country markets or price suppression or depression—have a temporal element built into them. That temporal lag means that serious prejudice cases likely cannot be brought until many years after the subsidies have allowed factories to become fully functional, selling their products in third-country markets in sufficient quantities to cause "displacement" of others, or with such sales occurring over a long enough period to observe a "depression" in prices. Add the time required to litigate a WTO dispute, and altogether it can take a complainant a minimum of five or six years to bring and win a subsidies challenge and achieve compliance.

THE INABILITY TO DISTINGUISH GOOD FROM BAD SUBSIDIES

Given the urgency of transitioning to clean energy and producing and promoting decarbonization technologies, countries around the world have increasingly turned to subsidies as one way to incentivize and scale up green technology development and installation. Despite agreement that subsidies hindering the fight against climate change (e.g., fossil fuel subsidies) should be disciplined, while those contributing to the deployment of renewable energy or decarbonization technologies should be encouraged, the WTO rules no longer provide any basis to distinguish between one type of subsidy and another.

When the rules were first established, the SCM Agreement contained a list of permitted ("non-actionable") subsidies for certain research activities, or disadvantaged regions, or adaptation to new environmental requirements, but consensus could not be reached to extend those provisions, so they lapsed on January 1, 2000.[37] However, in recent years, two new bases for distinguishing prohibited from permitted subsidies have entered the conversation. The 2022 Agreement on Fisheries Subsidies introduced the notion that subsidies could be prohibited based on their potential to undermine sustainable fishing practices, and that the SCM rules could be amended to further the United Nations' Sustainable Development Goals.[38] Similarly, the United States, Japan, and the EU launched discussions on the margins of the WTO's 2017 ministerial conference in Buenos Aires, Argentina, focused on adding trade- and market-distorting subsidies to the category of prohibited subsidies.[39] Although those trilateral discussions have not progressed to the stage of proposed changes to the SCM rules, they represent agreement among three major subsidy-granting jurisdictions that unlimited financial guarantees, certain direct debt forgiveness, and subsidies to certain insolvent enterprises or those in sectors with overcapacity need to be disciplined.

Today, many countries likely agree that a significant category exists of subsidies that are desirable and deserve policy space to flourish, including potentially those to address climate change or global health challenges, or development needs. However, defining those subsidies and agreeing on whether and how to carve them out of existing subsidy disciplines is a tall order, in part because subsidies often have various motivations—some of which are beneficial, such as addressing market failures, while others could be motivated by protectionism or simply lack a clear and up-to-date economic rationale. In addition, many subsidies are important social safety nets for the poor—designed to reduce the price for essential items such as food or heating oil or to keep people employed during economic crises—such that disciplining them could harm those most in need of government support.

THE U.S. CHALLENGE TO THE SUBSIDIES REGIME

The challenges posed to the international trading system from subsidies are not new. A 2006 report examining the link between subsidies, trade, and the WTO found that in 2003, just twenty-one developed countries spent $250 billion on subsidies, with total global spending estimated at $350 billion.[40] Some estimates even suggest global subsidies could total over $3 trillion a year, or about 4 percent of global gross domestic product (GDP) in 2006.[41] A more recent study found that since the global financial crisis, subsidies have been "the most frequent form of intervention . . . surpassing measures such as tariffs and other non-tariff measures," accounting for almost half of all interventions.[42] The spike in government spending is not limited to the financial crisis; subsidies have more than tripled since then.

Globally, the United States, China, and the European Union are responsible for more than half of all subsidy measures, prompting concerns over global equity, particularly regarding access to technology. In fact, a study by Global Trade Alert found that 37.6 percent of world trade in goods faced competitive distortions due to subsidies granted by the three largest markets to their own import-competing firms.[43] The breadth of those subsidies is also alarming. According to economists Simon J. Evenett and Johannes Fritz, before the start of the COVID-19 pandemic, "62% of global goods trade was in products and on trade routes where subsidised American, Chinese, and European firms compete."[44] Furthermore, 28 percent of all global goods are touched by U.S. and EU subsidies alone. Those numbers raise concerns about market access and fair competition globally.

Although governments have always used subsidies as tools to achieve certain policy aims, their proliferation over the last fifteen years is worrisome. A 2022 report by the OECD, the IMF, the World Bank, and the WTO found that "subsidies appear to be widespread, growing, and often poorly targeted at their intended policy objectives" and that "this situation is spurring the use of unilateral trade defense measures, eroding public support for open trade, and contributing to severe trade tensions that impede progress on other global trade priorities."[45] More recent and growing U.S. support for using subsidies and "Buy American" policies has amplified that concern. A good example of the latter is the Build America, Buy America Act, part of the Infrastructure Investment and Jobs Act of 2021, which includes a domestic content procurement preference for federal infrastructure projects. The Biden administration had to waive those requirements due to the complexity of implementing the local content rules, which many in the construction industry oppose.[46] However, in his 2023 State of the Union address, Biden doubled down on his Buy American plans and embraced what is being called a modern industrial strategy, irking U.S. trading partners and sowing fears of a global subsidies race.[47]

Two of the Biden administration's signature legislative initiatives, the IRA and the CHIPS and Science Act, provide a first look at the new industrial policy and highlight the challenges it could pose to international subsidy disciplines and U.S. trading relationships more broadly.

THE INFLATION REDUCTION ACT

The IRA is the Biden administration's signature climate action.[48] With $370 billion in spending and tax credits to fight climate change and invest in low-emission energy sources, the IRA aspires to reduce greenhouse gas emissions by 40 percent below 2005 levels by 2030. Its tax credits incentivize consumers to purchase electric vehicles (EVs) and green their homes, and utility companies to invest in cleaner energy sources such as wind and solar. Funds are also set aside for a "green bank" to invest in clean energy projects throughout the United States, focusing on poor communities, and oil and gas companies will now be subject to fees for excess methane leakage. The IRA is a broad spending package that Biden described as "the most significant investment ever to tackle the climate crisis."[49]

Though the IRA has generated bipartisan support, it has not been without controversy. Some U.S. allies, although welcoming of U.S. actions to do *something* on climate, have felt snubbed for not being consulted on certain provisions that discriminate against imports and prevent them from fully supporting the U.S. green transition. For example, one of the IRA's most discussed provisions includes a tax credit for consumers for certain qualifying electric vehicles that are assembled in the United States, Canada, or Mexico. Initially, that provision allowed a tax credit only for EVs assembled in the United States, but after a successful push from Canada and Mexico to account for the integrated North American auto supply chain, Congress adjusted the language.[50] However, the provision still looks like a local content requirement, which is prohibited under WTO subsidy rules—meaning Americans who choose to purchase EVs assembled in Japan, South Korea, or Europe would not be eligible for the tax credit. Of course, the devil is in the details of the implementing rules—which could allow some foreign components to be included in final assembly, for instance. In December 2022, the U.S. Department of the Treasury released a white paper outlining the direction of upcoming guidance on how the critical mineral and battery component would be calculated, suggesting flexibility in implementation.[51] Then, in April 2023, after receiving public comments, Treasury published a Notice of Proposed Rulemaking that further clarified that guidance.[52] The new rule relaxes the content requirements and includes general criteria for a "free trade agreement" partner, opening the way for Japanese manufacturers to benefit after USTR negotiated a deal with Japan on critical minerals.[53] The European Union and others are pushing for similar deals. However, those deals, and the new rule, remain contested.[54]

Another caveat to the EV tax credit is that for consumers to qualify for the entire $7,500 credit, the EV needs to include a battery in which 40 percent of the critical minerals and 50 percent of its components come from the United States or countries with which it has a trade agreement. That percentage will increase to 80 percent for critical minerals and 100 percent for components by 2029. The aim is to reduce reliance on China, which has 61 percent of the world's lithium refining capacity and 90 percent of anode and electrolyte production—both important battery components.[55] However, other countries have already been working toward securing critical mineral supply chains, and the United States does not have trade agreements with all of them. In particular, the EU, a major trading partner, would be excluded, though the Biden administration is attempting to ameliorate this gap with a critical minerals deal with select countries. European leaders are also concerned that U.S. spending will drive investment and jobs out of Europe and, more broadly, that "protectionism hinders competition and innovation and is detrimental to climate change mitigation."[56]

Before the IRA, the Biden administration claimed a bipartisan victory for industrial policy with the CHIPS and Science Act, which features a $52.7 billion investment in semiconductor manufacturing, research, and development, as well as workforce development.[57] Semiconductors are a critical component of the modern technological world; they power everything from smartphones to cars and washing machines to advanced weapons systems.

In the last eight years, U.S. semiconductor manufacturing capacity has declined by more than 10 percent.[58] The figure used by the Biden administration is that the U.S share of global semiconductor manufacturing has decreased from 37 percent in 1990 to just 12 percent in 2021.[59] Yet that widely cited figure only tells part of the story. A study by the Peterson Institute for International Economics notes that the U.S. share of global revenue from semiconductor manufacturing witnessed a much smaller decline in that same time period, from 25 to 20 percent.[60] In the design phase, the United States is still dominant, accounting for 46 percent of the market as of 2020.[61] Even so, although those firms are designing them in the United States, semiconductors are largely being made elsewhere.[62]

Taiwan is the global leader in semiconductor production, with 22 percent of the world's market share, followed by South Korea (21 percent), then Japan and China (at 15 percent each). Security concerns about Taiwan have only increased U.S. anxiety over market concentration and strengthened the push for a diversification strategy. Roughly 85 percent of advanced semiconductor chip production—those chips used primarily for smartphones, high-end computers, and military technologies—happens in Taiwan. In contrast, no advanced semiconductor chip production happens in the United States. For legacy semiconductor chip production (chips used in some vehicles and other consumer electronics), the United States accounts for 8 percent of total global production.[63]

Given how far behind the United States lags, building up a domestic semiconductor manufacturing base will be challenging and expensive. For example, over a ten-year period, the cost of ownership of a new manufacturing plant located in the United States is around 30 percent higher than in Singapore, South Korea, and Taiwan, and 37 to 50 percent higher than in China.[64]

Two aspects of the CHIPS and Science Act are of particular interest in the trade context. First are the geographical restrictions on funding.

Recipients of CHIPS and Science Act funds cannot direct those funds to expand manufacturing in China or a list of other countries considered a national security concern to the United States. Though China has proven to be a less attractive destination for U.S. investment in the semiconductor industry than Japan, Singapore, Taiwan, and Europe, the number of Chinese chips deals involving U.S. private investors has increased in recent years.[65]

Second, the spending blitz could be insufficient.[66] Taiwan is now spending $120 billion and has twenty new plants under construction or completed.[67] Korea has a $452 billion investment toward its own "K semiconductor belt strategy" to compete with Chinese and U.S. investments.[68] EU member states have also agreed to invest $44.4 billion to help reach their goal of producing 20 percent of the world's semiconductors by 2030.[69] India has invested $30 billion to bolster its domestic semiconductor and technology supply chains.[70] China, on the other hand—still reeling from the economic consequences of its COVID-19 lockdown strategy—has paused recent semiconductor investments, including a planned $145 billion investment, due to their high costs and disappointing results.[71]

The other issue to consider is that constructing new fabrication plants is a major endeavor, requiring massive resources and a tremendous amount of labor. For instance, Intel is currently building two facilities in Chandler, Arizona, for $20 billion, which is expected to take three years and five thousand skilled construction workers to complete.[72] Those investments could create many jobs and will require a skilled tech workforce to maintain over the long run.

Governments also face major challenges in subsidies' effectiveness due to the increasingly complex nature of the global semiconductor supply chain. Items needed for chipmaking come from many countries, with some critical minerals for the semiconductor supply chain originating in China.[73] Thus, subsidizing the domestic semiconductor industry within multiple countries could lead to the inefficient allocation of resources, and cooperation across countries will be necessary.

Furthermore, not only could those large investments and lack of international coordination lead to a supply glut of semiconductors, but they could also fail to solve the narrow market failure for which they seek to correct, and they could create unnecessary trade conflicts along the way.[74] The supply-chain disruptions brought on by the COVID-19 pandemic have minimized over time, and the high demand for semiconductor products has cooled down, which has led to a supply surplus and some companies scaling back their orders.[75]

Meanwhile, the United States and the European Union have mentioned their shared desire to avoid a subsidy race over semiconductors. However, existing dialogues, such as the Trade and Technology Council, could prove insufficient to avoid increasing disagreements between the United States and the EU.[76]

RECOMMENDATIONS

The United States has been consistently vocal about problems with international subsidy rules and the challenges to disciplining states, particularly China, that subvert those rules, while recognizing that the fight against climate change and pandemics requires major new government investment. To address both the concerns with and the opportunities created by industrial subsidies, the United States should pursue substantive reforms to the current regime, including rewriting the rules to better reflect current political and economic realities, promoting enhanced transparency, and urging penalties for noncompliance. Specifically, the United States should

- revisit what constitutes good and bad subsidies and propose limiting overall subsidy levels while carving out areas in the common international interest;

- encourage countries to disclose their subsidies, both by using the incentive of a "safe harbor" for subsidies that have been properly notified and enforcing penalties for those that consistently fail to make timely notifications of their subsidies; and

- strengthen the penalties for noncompliance with international subsidies rules.

Those recommendations address policy options achievable in the next year alongside discussions on WTO reform, as well as more substantive reforms to address deeper concerns with the rules themselves. Together, they suggest ways of retooling or rewriting existing measures in order to provide more flexibility to pursue legitimate objectives through subsidies—but also to more effectively rein in trade-distorting abuse of the system.

LIMIT AND DISTINGUISH HARMFUL SUBSIDIES

The WTO Agreement on Agriculture (AoA) offers some important lessons on how to consider the varied forms, amounts, and motivations for subsidies that should now apply to industrial subsidies. The AoA did something no other trade agreement and none of the SCM Agreement provisions has done: it limited the amount of financial support WTO members can provide for agricultural production. Members agreed to those limits because the magnitude of the then-existing subsidies, particularly the unsustainable $25 billion the EU and the United States spent annually on agricultural price supports in the 1980s, caused leading agricultural nations to perceive that "trade was gravely out of balance."[77]

The AoA works by dividing domestic support for agriculture into two basic categories: trade-distorting ("amber-box") subsidies, which can artificially raise or lower prices or stimulate production, and minimally trade-distorting ("green-box") subsidies, which do not unduly distort prices or production levels. Limits are imposed only on those amber-box subsidies considered trade-distorting. The AoA creates an additional distinction for production-limiting ("blue-box") programs not subject to the cap on total spending. The AoA permits all countries to participate in some level of subsidies by establishing de minimis levels of support that are permitted even though they are trade-distorting.[78]

Applying those lessons to industrial subsidies would involve

- launching negotiations immediately, under the auspices of the WTO or the OECD, to cap total spending on industrial subsidies;

- agreeing to some sublimits within that cap in the product sectors and supply-chain points with an observable concentration in subsidies;

- identifying a narrowly defined category of green-box subsidies without limits, such as for research and development, inspection and conformity, and disaster response; and

- agreeing to a list of blue-box subsidies that should be excluded from the overall cap because their contribution to the global common good outweighs their trade-distorting effects.

Ideally, the overall cap would be calculated as a percentage of total industrial output, optimally using an average for the total number of subsidies over a three-to-five-year period, given the significant swings in subsidies from year to year. Wealthy countries should be permitted to subsidize by a lower percentage than smaller, developing countries. As with the AoA, a new industrial subsidies regime should include transition periods geared to countries' levels of development and current levels of industrial subsidization. Finally, countries taking significant advantage of blue-box exclusions should commit to providing some measure of support, technical assistance, or technology transfers to developing countries in need of the global good to which the subsidies are directed. That arrangement could resemble the fund created in the WTO Agreement on Fisheries Subsidies, which provides technical assistance and capacity-building to developing-country members for implementing the agreement and uses the expertise of the United Nation's Food and Agriculture Organization, the International Fund for Agricultural Development, and the World Bank to do so.[79]

For industrial goods, among the subsidies that likely should be within the blue box are those that genuinely contribute to fighting climate change—for example, subsidies for renewable energy, carbon capture and sequestration, electric vehicles, and clean cooking stoves. Excluding subsidies that support global health from the cap, including essential medicines and medical equipment, will be equally important.[80] Subsidies that help ensure food and water access also deserve consideration. Many other areas need subsidies to stimulate investment in goods and services important to the global commons where market failures have caused underinvestment. Developing the list of which subsidies fall within the green or blue boxes will be one of the most difficult and most important elements of new subsidy disciplines. It should form the core of an expanded role for the WTO's SCM Committee. Examining those subsidies that can demonstrably help countries meet their Sustainable Development Goals would be a good place to start.

ENCOURAGE COUNTRIES TO REVEAL THEIR SUBSIDIES

Disciplines on subsidies will not work unless others are made aware promptly whenever subsidies are being granted. In order to encourage such transparency, the subsidy notification process should be reformed to

- develop clear guidance on exactly what should be notified as a subsidy, including which subsidies fall within the green or blue boxes;

- prohibit challenges to green or blue box subsidies for a period of at least one year;

- add penalties for failure to provide timely notifications of subsidies;

- treat non-notified subsidies as actionable and subject to immediate challenge unless the subsidy is proven unharmful to other members' trade interests; and

- incorporate independent information gathered by the WTO secretariat or provided by other members to fill any gaps in missing notifications.

Increased transparency should begin with making the notification process as easy and understandable as possible, with clear incentives for fulsome and timely notices. The WTO secretariat has begun that process through its shift to online tools, but more needs to be done, in conjunction with the SCM Committee, to ensure that all countries understand what they are required to notify and into which boxes their subsidies fall. A further incentive to notify immediately those subsidies that a country believes fall into the green box as non-trade-distorting (i.e., funds for basic research and development or disaster relief or the like) would be an agreement that subsidies notified as within the green box cannot be challenged at all or after a certain period of time, or until concerns over such subsidies have been raised and discussed at a meeting of the SCM Committee.[81] That safe harbor from challenge could be agreed upon as part of the notification process even without an agreement on overall caps on industrial subsidies.

Blue-box subsidies also deserve special notice and exemption from immediate challenge. Allowing countries to separately notify blue-box subsidies and explain why they are necessary to achieve important policy goals would provide the factual predicate for a safe harbor for such subsidies. Increased disclosures and discussions within the SCM Committee should also accompany blue-box subsidies in order to ensure that all members can understand the useful goods or technology derived from such government support. An additional onus should be placed on those claiming substantial exclusions for hefty blue-box subsidies to contribute to technical assistance or technology transfers to developing countries that need support in the area addressed by blue-box subsidies.

Countries for whom the safe-harbor incentives do not sufficiently prompt timely notifications should face penalties. Because the WTO lacks the authority to charge members monetary fines, penalties could take the form of depriving recalcitrant countries of certain privileges of WTO membership—such as access to meeting documents, oral interventions during formal meetings, the opportunity to chair WTO committees—or imposing the status of inactive member, an undesirable moniker for countries wishing to remain in good standing. A number of those penalty ideas are modeled on a 2017 proposal the United States submitted to the WTO.[82] Although some of the proposal's specifics came under attack, the underlying concept is a compelling one.[83] The Biden administration has since revised the proposal, and other members have supported it.[84] A further penalty would be to give countries the right to immediately challenge non-notified subsidies, even if they would otherwise be barred from such treatment because they fall into the green or blue boxes.

Finally, the WTO secretariat should be empowered to use the information collected on the newly established subsidy platform created by the IMF, OECD, World Bank, and the WTO to notify subsidies that seriously delinquent WTO members have failed to notify.[85] Making those subsidies part of the WTO's public record and subsidy database, underscoring that failure to disclose subsidies will not allow them to evade scrutiny, and providing additional technical support to countries that need assistance with their subsidy notifications should result in a more up to date and complete record of subsidy actions around the world.

INCREASE PENALTIES FOR RULES VIOLATIONS

A critical shortcoming of the current system is the inadequacy of remedies when subsidies violate the rules. Devising new mechanisms to enforce both the current rules and any agreed-upon new arrangements to address industrial subsidies' explosive growth will be important. To strengthen subsidies remedies, two changes are necessary: a speedier process for remedying subsidy rule violations and increased penalties for granting prohibited subsidies in the first place.

First, in order to shorten the time lag, now five to six years or more, between when a subsidy is granted and when a WTO panel can find that the subsidy violates the WTO's rules, the subsidy regime should borrow a page from the WTO Safeguards Agreement. Countries applying safeguard measures (typically tariffs or quotas) generally must pay for them by compensating those countries whose trade is harmed by the safeguards or, in the absence of an agreement on compensation, by permitting retaliation by harmed countries. The subsidies regime could do the same by allowing more immediate demands for compensation or the quick imposition of retaliatory measures. A similar proposal suggested by trade analysts Simon Lester, Inu Manak and Huan Zhu argues for establishing procedures to guard against abuse and to help determine the amount of rebalancing that would be permitted.[86] However, creating an additional category where immediate rebalancing is available would encourage compliance with new subsidy disciplines. In addition, the current expedited dispute settlement provisions for prohibited subsidies could be expanded to cover both existing and new prohibited subsidies, plus those subsidies not notified immediately to the WTO, so that a broader range of subsidy challenges could take advantage of the more truncated timeline for adjudicating subsidy disputes.[87]

Second, the penalty for violating subsidies disciplines could be substantially increased were the WTO to do what the European Union now does when it finds breaches of its anti-subsidy (called state-aid) rules: recipients of offending subsidies are required to pay back the entire amount of a subsidy.[88] Although that measure would substantially depart from the current WTO system, which was designed to preserve future trading opportunities rather than redress past injury, it is not totally unprecedented and would be consistent with EU practice.[89] At least one WTO panel came to the view that the only way to enforce the SCM prohibition on the grant or maintenance of export subsidies was to restore the situation to what it was before the subsidy was granted, which meant requiring that the grant be paid back in full.[90] Requiring the repayment of subsidies would be among the strongest deterrents to granting them in the first place. If retroactive remedies became the norm, the repayment requirement would presumably be limited to prohibited subsidies, making it essential that those subsidies be clearly defined.

CONCLUSION

Critics of the international subsidies regime fall into two camps—those who view existing rules as inflexible, limiting government action to address pressing policy issues, and those who view the rules as not stringent enough to avoid subsidy wars or trade conflicts. Both views are correct. Finding common ground between them has become all the more urgent as major economies increasingly turn to industrial policies to address both global concerns, such as fighting climate change and pandemics, and domestic competitiveness and supply-chain resilience needs. The good news is that there are many ways to revise and update subsidy rules to better balance competing priorities and take into account the fears in much of the developing world that its citizens will be left out and left behind. This report focuses on three methods: limiting and defining good versus bad subsidies, encouraging countries to reveal their subsidies, and improving enforcement through incentives for compliance and penalties for noncompliance.

Implicit in those recommendations is the message that rather than shunning the WTO, now is the time to better use its rules and tools. Those concerned about trade-distorting subsidies should challenge them at the WTO. However, the time has also come to have an honest conversation about the inadequacies in the current regime and options for a way forward. At its core, one of the WTO's critical roles is to help its members draw the line between protectionist measures and sound industrial policies, while ensuring that wherever that line is drawn, it does not unduly privilege some or harm others. To do that in the face of rising industrial polices across the globe, the WTO needs an updated toolbox.

Rethinking international trade rules on subsidies is a critical test for the United States too. The United States has led the charge against

China's rise on the back of massive subsidies and unwavering support for its state-owned enterprises, and it has begun doling out substantial subsidies of its own that flout the WTO rules barring the favoring of locally made goods. Thus, the United States should lead the effort to reshape the global rules to better serve its own interests and the international trading system's changing realities. Doing so would give the United States a powerful tool to address its twin concerns over competition with China and fighting climate change. It would also allow the WTO and the world to come closer to a more equitable, resilient, and sustainable international economic order.

ENDNOTES

1. This estimate includes spending for semiconductor manufacturing and research in the CHIPS and Science Act, climate and energy investments in the Inflation Reduction Act, and infrastructure spending under the Infrastructure Investment and Jobs Act. See Committee for a Responsible Federal Budget, "CBO Estimates 'Chips-Plus' Bill Would Cost $79 Billion," July 22, 2022, http://crfb.org/blogs/cbo-estimates-chips-plus-bill-would-cost-79-billion; Committee for a Responsible Federal Budget, "What's in the Inflation Reduction Act?," July 28, 2022, http://crfb.org/blogs/whats-inflation-reduction-act; Committee for a Responsible Federal Budget, "Infrastructure Plan Will Add $400 Billion to the Deficit, CBO Finds," August 5, 2021, http://crfb.org/blogs/infrastructure-plan-will-add-400-billion-deficit-cbo-finds; Ravi Agrawal, "The White House's Case for Industrial Policy," *Foreign Policy*, March 2, 2023. http://foreignpolicy.com/2023/03/02/live-industrial-policy-katherine-tai-trade-economy-chips-inflation.

2. Dani Rodrik, "Industrial Policy: Don't Ask Why, Ask How," *Middle East Development Journal* 1 (2009): 1–29, http://drodrik.scholar.harvard.edu/files/dani-rodrik/files/industrial-policy-dont-ask-why-ask-how.pdf.

3. Julius Krein, "What Alexandria Ocasio-Cortez and Marco Rubio Agree On," *New York Times*, August 20, 2019, http://nytimes.com/2019/08/20/opinion/america-industrial-policy.html.

4. Chad P. Bown, "COVID-19 Vaccine Supply Chains and the Defense Production Act," Peterson Institute for International Economics, Working Paper 22–9, June 2022, http://piie.com/publications/working-papers/covid-19-vaccine-supply-chains-and-defense-production-act.

5. Chad P. Bown, "China Bought None of the Extra $200 Billion of US Exports in Trump's Trade Deal," Peterson Institute for International Economics, July 19, 2022, http://piie.com/blogs/realtime-economic-issues-watch/china-bought-none-extra-200-billion-us-exports-trumps-trade.

6. Anshu Siripurapu and Noah Berman, "Is Industrial Policy Making a Comeback?," Council on Foreign Relations, November 2022, http://cfr.org/backgrounder/industrial-policy-making-comeback.

7. Alexander Hamilton, "Report on the Subject of Manufactures, December 5, 1791," in *Alexander Hamilton: Writings*, ed. Joanne B. Freeman (New York: Library of America, 2001), 692.

8. Douglas A. Irwin, "The Aftermath of Hamilton's "Report on Manufactures," *Journal of Economic History* 64, no. 3 (2004): 800–21.

9. Hamilton, "Report," 701.

10. See Andres B. Schwarzenberg, "Industrial Policy and International Trade," In Focus (Congressional Research Service), updated January 3, 2023, http://crsreports.congress .gov/product/pdf/IF/IF12119.

11. Brain Deese, "Remarks on Executing a Modern American Industrial Strategy by NEC Director Brian Deese," transcript of speech delivered at City Club of Cleveland, October 13, 2022, http://wita.org/trade-news/remarks-on-industrial-strategy.

12. White House, "Remarks of President Joe Biden—State of the Union Address as Prepared for Delivery," February 7, 2023, http://whitehouse.gov/briefing-room /speeches-remarks/2023/02/07/remarks-of-president-joe-biden-state-of-the-union -address-as-prepared-for-delivery.

13. National Science and Technology Council, National Strategy for Advanced Manufacturing, October 2022, 1, http://whitehouse.gov/wp-content/uploads/2022/10/National -Strategy-for-Advanced-Manufacturing-10072022.pdf.

14. Deese, "Remarks."

15. Gina M. Raimondo, "Remarks by U.S. Secretary of Commerce Gina Raimondo on the U.S. Competitiveness and the China Challenge," U.S. Department of Commerce, November 30, 2022, http://commerce.gov/news/speeches/2022/11/remarks-us -secretary-commerce-gina-raimondo-us-competitiveness-and-china.

16. Andrea Shalal, "Yellen Says Lowering U.S. Tariffs on Chinese Goods 'Worth Considering,'" Reuters, April 22, 2022, http://reuters.com/business/yellen-says -lowering-us-tariffs-chinese-goods-worth-considering-2022-04-22; Janet Yellen, "Remarks by Secretary of the Treasury Janet L. Yellen at Bilateral Meeting With People's Republic of China Vice Premier Liu He," U.S. Department of the Treasury, January 18, 2023, http://home.treasury.gov/news/press-releases/jy1191.

17. Katherine Tai, Review of the Activities and Fiscal Year 2022 Funding Priorities of the Office of the U.S. Trade Representative, Before the S. Comm. on Appropriations, April 28, 2021, http://appropriations.senate.gov/hearings/review-of-the-activities -and-fiscal-year-2022-funding-priorities-of-the-office-of-the-us-trade-representative-.

18. Dan Dupont, "Tai: U.S. Must 'Keep Replicating' CHIPS Act Efforts for Other Industries," Inside U.S. Trade, August 8, 2022, http://insidetrade.com/daily-news/tai -us-must-'keep-replicating'-chips-act-efforts-other-industries.

19. White House, "Fact Sheet: President Biden Sets 2030 Greenhouse Gas Pollution Reduction Target Aimed at Creating Good-Paying Union Jobs and Securing U.S. Leadership on Clean Energy Technologies," April 22, 2021, http://whitehouse.gov /briefing-room/statements-releases/2021/04/22/fact-sheet-president-biden-sets-2030 -greenhouse-gas-pollution-reduction-target-aimed-at-creating-good-paying-union-jobs -and-securing-u-s-leadership-on-clean-energy-technologies.

20. Doug Palmer, "Biden 'Confident' U.S. Can Address EU Concerns About IRA Subsidies," *Politico*, December 1, 2022, http://politico.com/news/2022/12/01/biden-eu-ira-subsidies-00071645.

21. Kristalina Georgieva, Vitor Gaspar, and Ceyla Pazarbasioglu, "Poor and Vulnerable Countries Need Support to Adapt to Climate Change," International Monetary Fund, March 23, 2022, http://imf.org/en/Blogs/Articles/2022/03/23/blog032322-poor-and-vulnerable-countris-need-support-to-adapt-to-climate-change.

22. Margrethe Vestager, "Speech by Executive Vice-President Margrethe Vestager in the State Aid High Level Forum of Member States," European Commission, January 2023, http://ec.europa.eu/commission/presscorner/detail/en/speech_23_1971.

23. Anne O. Krueger, "Sleepwalking Into a Global Trade War," Project Syndicate, December 22, 2022, http://project-syndicate.org/commentary/trade-world-war-us-subsidies-protectionism-by-anne-o-krueger-2022-12.

24. Agrawal, "White House's Case."

25. International Monetary Fund, Organization for Economic Cooperation and Development, World Bank, and World Trade Organization, *Subsidies, Trade, and International Cooperation*, April 22, 2022, http://wto.org/english/news_e/news22_e/igo_22apr22_e.pdf.

26. Andrew L. Stoler, "Evolution of Subsidies Disciplines in GATT and the WTO," *Journal of World Trade* 44, no. 4 (2010): 797, http://kluwerlawonline.com/journalarticle/Journal+of+World+Trade/44.4/TRAD2010030.

27. World Trade Organization, "Agreement on Interpretation and Application of Articles VI, XVI and XXIII of the General Agreement on Tariffs and Trade," April 12, 1979, http://wto.org/english/docs_e/legal_e/tokyo_scm_e.pdf.

28. John D. Greenwald, "Negotiating Subsidies in the GATT/WTO: The Tokyo Round," in *What Shapes the Law? Reflections on the History, Law, Politics and Economics of International and European Subsidy Disciplines*, ed. Luca Rubini and Jennifer Hawkins (Florence: European University Institute, 2016), 37–39, http://ueaeprints.uea.ac.uk/id/eprint/60598/1/WhatShapesLaw_2016.pdf.

29. J. Michael Finger and Julio Nogués, "International Control of Subsidies and Countervailing Duties," *World Bank Economic Review* 1, no. 4 (1987): 707–25, http://jstor.org/stable/3989907, 713.

30. See World Trade Organization, Report of the Working Party on the Accession of China, WT/ACC/CHN/49, October 1, 2001, 9 (paragraph 46), http://docs.wto.org/dol2fe/Pages/SS/directdoc.aspx?filename=Q:/WT/ACC/CHN49.pdf&Open=True.

31. Henry Gao and Weihuan Zhou, *Between Market Economy and State Capitalism: China's State-Owned Enterprises and the World Trading System* (Cambridge: Cambridge University Press, 2022).

32. Prior to 2007, the United States did not apply its CVD law to countries considered to be nonmarket economies (NMEs) based in part on a conclusion by the Department of Commerce that it could not determine where government action began or ended and therefore could not specifically identify subsidies, a conclusion that was upheld in a court challenge (*Georgetown Steel Corp. v. United States*, 801 F.2d 1308 (Fed. Cir. 1986)). In 2006, Commerce changed its position, distinguishing the current

Chinese economy from the Soviet-style economies that had prompted the original determination that CVDs could not be found in NMEs. Numerous CVD cases followed, with eighty CVD orders now in place against imports from China.

33. World Trade Organization Appellate Body, United States—Definitive Anti-dumping and Countervailing Duties on Certain Products From China, WT/DS379/AB/R, March 11, 2011, http://docs.wto.org/dol2fe/Pages/SS/directdoc.aspx?filename=Q:/WT/DS/379ABR.pdf&Open=True.

34. World Trade Organization, Agreement on Subsidies and Countervailing Measures, Marrakesh Agreement Establishing the World Trade Organization, April 15, 1994, Annex 1A, 1869 U.N.T.S. 14 (hereinafter SCM Agreement), Article 25, http://wto.org/english/docs_e/legal_e/24-scm.pdf.

35. See subsidydata.org.

36. SCM Agreement, Article 4.7.

37. SCM Agreement, Article 8.2.

38. Ngozi Okonjo-Iweala, "Fisheries subsidies deal will contribute to sustainable blue economy: DG Okonjo-Iweala," World Trade Organization, June 28, 2022, http://wto.org/english/news_e/spno_e/spno28_e.htm.

39. Cecilia Malmstrom et al., "Joint Statement by the United States, European Union and Japan at MC11," Office of the U.S. Trade Representative, December 12, 2017, http://ustr.gov/about-us/policy-offices/press-office/press-releases/2017/december/joint-statement-united-states. They proposed adding four new types of subsidies to the prohibited list: unlimited guarantees, subsidies to an insolvent or ailing enterprise in the absence of a credible restructuring plan, subsidies to enterprises unable to obtain long-term financing or investment from independent commercial sources operating in sectors or industries in overcapacity, and certain direct forgiveness of debt. See Office of the U.S. Trade Representative, "Joint Statement of the Trilateral Meeting of the Trade Ministers of Japan, the United States and the European Union," January 14, 2020, http://ustr.gov/about-us/policy-offices/press-office/press-releases/2020/january/joint-statement-trilateral-meeting-trade-ministers-japan-united-states-and-european-union.

40. World Trade Organization, *World Trade Report 2006: Exploring the Links Between Subsidies, Trade and the WTO, Annual Report, 2006,* http://wto.org/english/res_e/booksp_e/anrep_e/world_trade_report06_e.pdf.

41. World Trade Organization, *World Trade Report 2006,* 45.

42. IMF et al., Subsidies, Trade, and International Cooperation.

43. Simon J. Evenett and Johannes Fritz, *Subsidies and Market Access: Towards an Inventory of Corporate Subsidies by China, the European Union and the United States, 28th Global Trade Alert Report* (London: Centre for Economic Policy Research, 2021), http://globaltradealert.org/reports/gta-28-report.

44. Evenett and Fritz, *Subsidies and Market Access,* 6.

45. IMF et al., Subsidies, Trade, and International Cooperation.

46. Colin Grabow, "Biden Administration Tacitly Admits Buy America Requirements Are Hindering Efforts to Improve Infrastructure," Cato Institute, May 25, 2022, http://

cato.org/blog/buy-america-requirements-already-proving-hindrance-improving
-infrastructure.

47. Daniel W. Drezner, "Quick Hits on the 2023 State of the Union Speech," *Drezner's World* (blog), February 7, 2023, http://danieldrezner.substack.com/p/quick-hits-on-the-2023-state-of-the.

48. All of the IRA's eight titles include provisions to address climate change, though the bill also includes issues related to health care and taxation.

49. White House, "Remarks of President Joe Biden."

50. Keith Nuthall, "Canadian Auto Sector Praises Tax-Credit Extension for U.S.-Made EVs," WardsAuto, August 2, 2022, http://wardsauto.com/industry-news/canadian-auto-sector-praises-tax-credit-extension-us-made-evs.

51. Department of Treasury, "Anticipated Direction of Forthcoming Proposed Guidance on Critical Mineral and Battery Component Value Calculations for the New Clean Vehicle Credit," December 29, 2022, http://home.treasury.gov/system/files/136/30DWhite-Paper.pdf.

52. Federal Register, Internal Revenue Service (IRS), Treasury, Notice of Proposed Rulemaking, 88 FR 23370, 4/17/2023, http://federalregister.gov/documents/2023/04/17/2023-06822/section-30d-new-clean-vehicle-credit.

53. Chad Bown, "Industrial Policy for Electric Vehicle Supply Chains and the U.S.-EU Fight Over the Inflation Reduction Act," Peterson Institute for International Economics, Working Paper 23-1, May 2023, http://piie.com/sites/default/files/2023-05/wp23-1.pdf.

54. Inu Manak, "Biden Is Rewriting the Rules on Trade—and Americans Should Be Worried," *Foreign Policy*, April 28, 2023, http://foreignpolicy.com/2023/04/28/ira-trade-ustr-tai-biden-congress-fta.

55. Chad P. Bown and Kristin Dziczek, "Why U.S. Allies Are Upset Over Electric Vehicle Subsidies in the Inflation Reduction Act," Peterson Institute for International Economics, October 3, 2022, http://piie.com/blogs/realtime-economics/why-us-allies-are-upset-over-electric-vehicle-subsidies-inflation; Veronika Henze, "China's Battery Supply Chain Tops BNEF Ranking for Third Consecutive Time, With Canada a Close Second," BloombergNEF, November 12, 2022, http://about.bnef.com/blog/chinas-battery-supply-chain-tops-bnef-ranking-for-third-consecutive-time-with-canada-a-close-second.

56. Eshe Nelson, "At Davos, European Distress Over a 'Made in America' Law," *New York Times*, January 21, 2023, http://nytimes.com/2023/01/21/business/davos-europe-inflation-reduction-act.html.

57. White House, "Fact Sheet: CHIPS and Science Act Will Lower Costs, Create Jobs, Strengthen Supply Chains, and Counter China," August 9, 2022, http://whitehouse.gov/briefing-room/statements-releases/2022/08/09/fact-sheet-chips-and-science-act-will-lower-costs-create-jobs-strengthen-supply-chains-and-counter-china. CHIPS stands for "creating helpful incentives to produce semiconductors."

58. Semiconductor Industry Association, "2022 Factbook," accessed April 2, 2023, http://semiconductors.org/wp-content/uploads/2022/05/SIA-2022-Factbook_df.

59. White House, "Fact Sheet: Biden-Harris Administration Bringing Semiconductor Manufacturing Back to America," January 21, 2022, http://whitehouse.gov/briefing-room/statements-releases/2022/01/21/fact-sheet-biden-harris-administration-bringing-semiconductor-manufacturing-back-to-america-2.

60. Gary Clyde Hufbauer and Megan Hogan, "CHIPS Act Will Spur US Production but Not Foreclose China," Peterson Institute for International Economics, October 2022, http://piie.com/sites/default/files/2022-10/pb22-13.pdf.

61. Ramiro Palma et al., "The Growing Challenge of Semiconductor Design Leadership," Semiconductor Industry Association, November 2022, http://semiconductors.org/the-growing-challenge-of-semiconductor-design-leadership.

62. Will Knight, "The US Needs to Get Back in the Business of Making Chips," *Wired*, July 14, 2021, http://wired.com/story/us-needs-back-business-making-chips.

63. Kathrin Hille and Demetri Sevastopulo, "TSMC: The Taiwanese Chipmaker Caught Up in the Tech Cold War," *Financial Times*, October 24, 2022, http://ft.com/content/bae9756a-3bce-4595-b6c9-8082fd735aa0; Will Hunt, "Sustaining U.S. Competitiveness in Semiconductor Manufacturing," Center for Security and Emerging Technology, January 2022; http://cset.georgetown.edu/publication/sustaining-u-s-competitiveness-in-semiconductor-manufacturing.

64. Antonio Varas et al., "Government Incentives and U.S. Competitiveness in Semiconductor Manufacturing," Semiconductor Industry Association, September 2020, http://semiconductors.org/wp-content/uploads/2020/09/Government-Incentives-and-US-Competitiveness-in-Semiconductor-Manufacturing-Sep-2020.pdf.

65. Semiconductor Industry Association, "2022: State of the U.S. Semiconductor Industry," accessed April 2, 2023, http://semiconductors.org/wp-content/uploads/2022/11/SIA_State-of-Industry-Report_Nov-2022.pdf. See also Kate O'Keeffe, Heather Somerville, and Yang Jie, "U.S. Companies Aid China's Bid for Chip Dominance Despite Security Concerns," *Wall Street Journal*, November 12, 2021, http://wsj.com/articles/u-s-firms-aid-chinas-bid-for-chip-dominance-despite-security-concerns-11636718400.

66. Vishnu Kannan and Jacob Feldgoise, "After the CHIPS Act: The Limits of Reshoring and Next Steps for U.S. Semiconductor Policy," Carnegie Endowment for International Peace, November 22, 2022, http://carnegieendowment.org/2022/11/22/after-chips-act-limits-of-reshoring-and-next-steps-for-u.s.-semiconductor-policy-pub-88439.

67. Yu Nakamura and Hideaki Ryugen, "What Taiwan Risk? Island's Chipmakers Embark on $120bn Buildup," Nikkei Asia, June 14, 2022, http://asia.nikkei.com/Business/Tech/Semiconductors/What-Taiwan-risk-Island-s-chipmakers-embark-on-120bn-buildup.

68. Sohee Kim and Sam Kim, "Korea Unveils $450 Billion Push for Global Chipmaking Crown," Bloomberg News, May 13, 2021, http://bloomberg.com/news/articles/2021-05-13/korea-unveils-450-billion-push-to-seize-global-chipmaking-crown.

69. Jillian Deutsch, "EU Nations Advance €43 Billion Plan to Become Semiconductor Hub," Bloomberg News, November 23, 2022, http://bloomberg.com/news/articles/2022-11-23/eu-nations-advance-43-billion-plan-to-become-semiconductor-hub.

70. Cheng Ting-Fang and Lauly Li, "The Resilience Myth: Fatal Flaws in the Push to Secure Chip Supply Chains," *Financial Times*, August 4, 2022, http://ft.com/content/f76534bf-b501-4cbf-9a46-80be9feb670c.

71. Bloomberg News, "Battered by Covid, China Hits Pause on Giant Chip Spending Aimed at Rivaling U.S.," January 3, 2023, http://bloomberg.com/news/articles/2023 -01-04/battered-by-covid-china-hits-pause-on-giant-chip-spending.

72. Don Clark, "The Huge Endeavor to Produce a Tiny Microchip," *New York Times*, April 8, 2022, http://nytimes.com/2022/04/08/technology/intel-chip-shortage.html.

73. Ting-Fang and Li, "Resilience Myth."

74. Scott Lincicome and Ilana Blumsack, "The Top Seven Reasons to Oppose New Semi-conductor Subsidies," Cato Institute, December 17, 2021, http://cato.org/blog/top -seven-reasons-oppose-new-semiconductor-subsidies; Fred Ashton, "Hold the CHIPS: The Private Sector Is Fixing the Semiconductor Shortage," American Action Forum, July 25, 2022, http://americanactionforum.org/insight/hold-the-chips-the-private -sector-is-fixing-the-semiconductor-shortage.

75. Dan Gallagher, "Micron Rains on Government's Chip Parade," *Wall Street Journal*, August 9, 2022, http://wsj.com/articles/micron-rains-on-governments-chip-parade -11660067632?mod=djemheard_t; Don Clark, "Chip Makers, Once in High Demand, Confront Sudden Challenges," *New York Times*, October 27, 2022, http://nytimes.com /2022/10/27/technology/chip-makers-challenges.html.

76. Sujai Shivakumar, Charles Wessner, and Thomas Howell, "Opportunities and Pitfalls for U.S.-EU Collaboration on Semiconductor Value Chain Resilience," Center for Strategic and International Studies, July 7, 2022, http://csis.org/analysis/opportunities -and-pitfalls-us-eu-collaboration-semiconductor-value-chain-resilience.

77. Jane M. Porter and Douglas E. Bowers, *A Short History of U.S. Agricultural Trade Negotiations* (Washington: U.S. Department of Agriculture, Economic Research Service, Agriculture and Rural Economy Division, 1989), 19.

78. World Trade Organization, "Agreement on Agriculture," January 1, 1995, http://wto .org/english/docs_e/legal_e/14-ag.pdf; World Trade Organization, "Domestic Support in Agriculture: The Boxes," accessed April 4, 2023, http://wto.org/english/tratop_e /agric_e/agboxes_e.htm.

79. World Trade Organization, Fisheries Subsidies—Establishment of a WTO Funding Mechanism to Finance Technical Assistance and Capacity Building in Support of Implementation of New WTO Fisheries Subsidies Disciplines, TN/C/21/Rev.1, June 5, 2022, http://docs.wto.org/dol2fe/Pages/SS/directdoc.aspx?filename=q:/TN/C/21R1 .pdf&Open=True.

80. Chad P. Bown and Thomas J. Bollyky, "The World Needs a COVID-19 Vaccine Investment and Trade Agreement," Peterson Institute for International Economics, October 13, 2021, http://piie.com/blogs/trade-and-investment-policy-watch/world-needs-covid -19-vaccine-investment-and-trade-agreement.

81. This could be structured similarly to the now expired Article 8 provisions of the SCM agreement, which were considered nonactionable.

82. World Trade Organization, *Procedures to Enhance Transparency and Strengthen Notification Requirements Under WTO Agreements, Communication From the United States*, JOB/GC/148, October 30, 2017, http://docs.wto.org/dol2fe/Pages/SS/directdoc.aspx ?filename=q:/Jobs/GC/148.pdf&Open=True.

83. Inu Manak, "The U.S. Pushes for Penalties on Failure to Notify at the WTO," *International Economic Law and Policy Blog*, November 14, 2017, http://worldtradelaw .typepad.com/ielpblog/2017/11/the-us-pushes-for-penalties-on-failure-to-notify-at -the-wto.html.

84. World Trade Organization, "Procedures to Enhance Transparency and Strengthen Notification Requirements Under WTO Agreements, Communication From Argentina, Australia, Canada, Costa Rica, the European Union, Israel, Japan, New Zealand, the Separate Customs Territory of Taiwan, Penghu, Kinmen and Matsu, United Kingdom, and the United States," June 25, 2021, http://docs.wto.org/dol2fe/Pages/SS/directdoc. aspx?filename=q:/Jobs/GC/204R5.pdf&Open=True

85. See subsidydata.org.

86. Simon Lester and Huan Zhu, "A Proposal for 'Rebalancing' to Deal with 'National Security' Trade Restrictions," *Fordham International Law Journal*, Vol, 42, Issue 5, 2019; Simon Lester and Inu Manak, "A Proposal for a Committee on National Security at the WTO,"30 *Duke Journal of Comparative & International Law* 267-281 (2020), http:// scholarship.law.duke.edu/djcil/vol30/iss2/3.

87. Article 4 of WTO Agreement on Subsidies and Countervailing Measures.

88. See Luca Rubini, *The Definition of Subsidy and State Aid: WTO and EC Law in Comparative Perspective* (Oxford: Oxford University Press, 2009); and Ilze Jozepa, EU State Aid Rules and WTO Subsidies Agreement, House of Commons Library, August 4, 2021, http:// researchbriefings.parliament.uk/ResearchBriefing/Summary/SN06775.

89. Luca Rubini, *The Definition of Subsidy and State Aid: WTO and EC Law in Comparative Perspective* (Oxford: Oxford University Press, 2009).

90. Australia–Automotive Leather, WT/DS/126/RW, adopted February 11, 2000. See also Tasi-yu Liu, "Remedies for Export Subsidies in the Context of Article 4 of the SCM Agreement: Rethinking Some Persistent Issues," *Asian Journal of WTO and International Health Law and Policy* 3 (2008): 21–50.

ABOUT THE AUTHORS

Jennifer A. Hillman is a senior fellow for trade and international political economy at the Council on Foreign Relations, a professor at the Georgetown University Law Center, and the codirector of Georgetown Law's Center on Inclusive Trade and Development. Her work has focused on the rules-based trading system and its implications for everything from climate change to Brexit and from China's Belt and Road Initiative to critically needed reforms at the World Trade Organization (WTO). In 2012, Hillman completed her term as one of seven members serving on the WTO's highest court, its Appellate Body. As a commissioner at the U.S. International Trade Commission, she adjudicated trade remedy and intellectual property cases along with conducting trade-related economic studies. Through her work as general counsel at the Office of the U.S. Trade Representative, Hillman was involved in all litigation matters coming before panels of the North American Free Trade Agreement (NAFTA) or the WTO. She negotiated bilateral agreements with forty-five countries while serving as the U.S. Trade Representative's ambassador and chief textiles negotiator.

Before joining the Office of the USTR, she was the legislative director for U.S. Senator Terry Sanford of North Carolina. Hillman was a partner in the law firm of Cassidy Levy Kent, a senior transatlantic fellow for the German Marshall Fund of the United States, and a member of the selection panel for the Harry Truman Scholarship Foundation. Hillman coauthored the CFR Independent Task Force report *China'sBelt and Road: Implications for the United States* (2021). She has also published two books drawn from seminars she co-taught at Georgetown Law: *Legal Aspects of Brexit: Implications of the United*

Kingdom's Decision to Withdraw From the European Union and *Getting to Brexit: Legal Aspects of the Process of the UK's Withdrawal From the EU*. She is a graduate of Duke University and Harvard Law School.

Inu Manak is a fellow for trade policy at the Council on Foreign Relations. An expert in international political economy, Manak's research focuses on U.S. trade policy and the law and politics of the World Trade Organization. Her recent book, *The Development Dimension: Special and Differential Treatment in Trade* was coauthored with James Bacchus, the first chairman of the WTO's Appellate Body. Manak was most recently a research fellow at the Cato Institute's Herbert A. Stiefel Center for Trade Policy Studies. Before joining the Cato Institute, she was a junior visiting fellow at the Graduate Institute's Centre for Trade and Economic Integration and a fellow at TradeLab, a Geneva-based nongovernmental organization (NGO) that helps developing countries, subject-matter experts, and NGOs build legal capacity in trade and investment law.

Manak is a book review editor for *World Trade Review* and a participating scholar in the Robert A. Pastor North America Research Initiative, a joint program between American University's Center for Latin American and Latino Studies and School of International Service. She also serves on the executive board for the TradeExperettes and the advisory board of Georgetown Law's Center on Inclusive Trade and Development. She received a BA in political science from Simon Fraser University, an MA in international affairs from American University's School of International Service, and a PhD in government from Georgetown University.

ADVISORY COMMITTEE

Rethinking International Rules on Subsidies

This report reflects the judgments and recommendations of the author. It does not necessarily represent the views of members of the advisory committee, whose involvement should in no way be interpreted as an endorsement of the report by either themselves or the organizations with which they are affiliated.